Nantucket Cat Tales

Nantucket Cat Tales

An Anthology
Edited by Caroline Daniels

Stories by
Loren Brock
Caroline Daniels
John Daniels
Lisa Penn Dias
Emily Etheridge
Danielle Frommer
Beverly Hall
Jan Jaeger
Mary Miles
Nantucket Junior Girl Scout Troop 995
Nancy Simonton
Lynn Tucker

Illustrations by
Caroline Daniels
Carol Petit
Jozie Thompson

Profits from this book support the
Nantucket Cat Rescue Fund

Whales' Tales

Published by
Whales' Tales Children's Books
Nantucket, MA
2000

Whales' Tales

Whales' Tales Children's Books
19 North Pasture Lane
Nantucket, MA 02554
(508) 228-4885
(508) 325-4256
Copyright © 2000
Caroline Daniels, Lisa Dias
on behalf of the Nantucket Cat Rescue Fund
Printed in the United States of America
First Whales' Tales Children's Books Edition, 2000.
Copyright information and acknowledgements are continued on pages 1-5.
ISBN 0-9673199-0-0
Library of Congress

Nantucket
Cat Tales

Contents

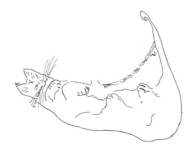

About the Authors and Illustrators

Loren Brock is the owner of The Toy Boat, a unique children's toy and book shop on Straight Wharf. Loren volunteers with Nantucket Cat Rescue as our "Placement Director" for kittens and cats found by Nantucket Cat Rescue and/or placed with the Nantucket MSPCA shelter.
"Liv" © Loren Brock, 2000.

Dr. N. Caroline Daniels is a writer of both fiction and non-fiction. Her publishing company, Whales' Tales Children's Books, focuses on children's books and books that will benefit animal life and the environment. Caroline is one of the founders of Nantucket Cat Rescue, along with Lisa Dias, Margaret Frommer, and Cindy Reis Gordon.
"How Cats Came to Nantucket"
© N. Caroline Daniels, 2000.

John L. Daniels is a poet, vice-president for IBM, and an avid golfer. He is the author of several books about information technology. He lives with his wife, Caroline, son Jake and ten+ cats in Nantucket and Dedham, Massachusetts.

Lisa Penn Dias works at The Wauwinet Inn as the Guest Services Manager. Lisa is one of the founders of Nantucket Cat Rescue and is passionate about the spay/neuter, release program, and has been able to witness, first-hand, the long-term benefits by observing the feral colony she and her husband, Kenny, manages.

Emily Etheridge is a Summer visitor to Nantucket and considers Nantucket her second home. She is six years old and will go to first grade in September, 2000. She has very special Grand Parents who gave her a special kitten.
"Cleo" © Emily Etheridge, 2000.
"Cleo" Illustration. © Emily Etheridge, 2000.

Danielle Frommer is a long time resident of Nantucket, always active in rescuing and caring for the cat population. She has instilled the love of cats in her eight children, all of whom have multiple cat households.
"Pickles" © Danielle Frommer, 2000.

Beverly Hall is an internationally acclaimed, and much loved, Nantucket photographer, and a long time lover of cats. Her portrait work is world renown. She generously donated funds to build a special shelter area at the Nantucket MSPCA which is a quiet place for animals to recuperate. Nantucket Cat Rescue uses these quarters on a regular basis.
"A Passion for Orange" © Beverly Hall, 2000.
"The F.B.I. Cat" © Beverly Hall, 2000.

Jan Jaeger is the owner of Geronimo's, Nantucket's pet supply, gift, and grooming shop. Her pets at home are Junior, a Chesapeake Bay Retriever, and three cats named Jezebel, Jetti, and Miz Edna. She writes a column called "Pet Perspectives," each week for the "Inquirer and Mirror," Nantucket's newspaper, where all of her material contributed here was originally published.

"Cats in Our Language" © Jan Jaeger, 2000.

"Prodigal Kitty" © Jan Jaeger, 2000.

"What's Your Cat's Sign" © Jan Jaeger, 2000.

"Rules Our Cats Live By" © Jan Jaeger, 2000.

Mary Miles is a writer for "Yesterday's Island," has written for Cape Cod Magazine, and the "Inquirer and Mirror," and is the author of several children's books. She lives in Nantucket with her cat, Thistle.

"It's George, By George" © Mary Miles, 2000.

"Her Royal Highness Thistle" © Mary Miles, 2000.

Nantucket Junior Girl Scout Troop 995 is a group of young women interested in animal life and the environment. Their troop leader, Gail Ellis, is a cat rescue supporter.

Carol Petit is an artist and animal lover, living in Nantucket. She concentrates on drawing and pastel portraits, with some work in acrylics and oils, and is now spending more time exploring watercolor. She is a member of the Artists' Association of Nantucket and the Fuller Museum of Art.

Cover Illustration © Carol Petit, 2000.

Nancy Simonton lived in Nantucket for 6 1/2 years and worked for THE BEACON as the office manager, contributing a few articles. She now lives in Maine with her husband, Ward, on a farm that they are restoring. She has five cats: Momma and BB, Critter, Nubbin, and Goose.
"Momma and BB" © Nancy Simonton, 2000

Jozie Thompson is a Nantucket native and lives on island over her ten stall barn with her wonderhorse, Maynard, 2 dogs, 6 cats, and a fish named "Bob." Jozie is an artist and illustrator who has illustrated two children's books.
"The Charmer" Illustration.
© Jozie Thompson, 2000.
"Nantucket Cat Tails" Illustration.
© Jozie Thompson, 2000.

Lynn Tucker is a skin care and body therapist, and the owner of Body Treatments, services, and bath care products company. She's lived on Nantucket for 14 years and is a devoted animal lover. She lives with her Golden Retriever Cozner.
"Sammy Tucker" © Lynn Tucker, 2000.

Preface

A number of wonderful people have contributed to put this book together. The tales are enjoyable and illustrate the warmth of the human and feline hearts. We certainly hope you smile and relax while reading the stories, since they reflect a shared love of cats in the Nantucket Community.

The purpose of the book is to support the community effort to humanely manage the cat population on Nantucket. Therefore, we have to deliver a short, yet bitter message, before letting you go on to enjoy the book.

The species of cat we recognize as the common house cat was bred to live in a human environment. Cats, including feral cats, are not able to survive well without human beings. They starve, they dehydrate, their life expectancies are cut short to a year or two of hardship. It is a painful and horrible existence.

Feral cats are domestic cats that are lost or abandoned. Unless they are spayed or neutered, they reproduce. Kittens that are left to grow up without human contact become afraid of human contact. They live out a life that fits the description above.

The good news is that we, as a community, are doing something positive about it. During the winter of 1998/1999, while the powerful Northeasters were pummeling the island, a few concerned Nantucketers congregated. When that happens, ideas are cultivated, maps drawn, journeys plotted, and plans laid out. We formed Nantucket Cat Rescue to manage the feral cat population on the island and to offer education and support to cat owners.

The program is successful. During the first year of operation, from June 1, 1999 through May 31, 2000 over 200 cats were spayed and neutered. The overall feral cat population has been significantly reduced, while socialized kittens, cats, including some strays, have been homed.

How is this made possible?
  • *We had a good plan to start that emphasizes community, grass roots involvement.* Numerous people have kept their eyes open, located cats, trapped them, and delivered them to the Vets to be spayed, neutered, and treated for health issues. Volunteers fostered kittens, giving a great deal of time to get kittens used to human company, socializing them for adoption. More volunteers continue to provide food and shelter for colonies of spayed/neutered, healthy cats that could not be socialized so that they can live out their feral existence with a higher quality of life.

- *The Nantucket MSPCA, a dedicated and concerned staff, with the guidance of Judy Clarkson as Program Director and Dr. Paula Klek as head Veterinarian, did everything they could do to make this program work.* The technicians looked after the cats with care, the front desk people cleared the paperwork quickly and made us feel welcome, the Vets treated the cats attentively. The shelter staff worked to get socialized kittens and cats adopted successfully. The administration in Boston helped to create a structure that would work. In September, Nantucket Cat Rescue received a President's award from the MSPCA's Gus Thornton that indicated to us the level of support and cooperation for the program. Everyone went above and beyond the call.
- Dr. Sherry Holt provides care and advice to feral cats for colony owners.
- *Funding.* We had a very generous, anonymous, gift of $10,000 which took us through our first year allowing us to concentrate on cat welfare completely, rather than worry about funding. To that cat person and family, we would like to say a very large THANK YOU!

We have continuing support for funding from individuals AND IT DOES MAKE A DIFFERENCE! To everyone, THANK YOU! Please continue sending the cards and messages, it helps a lot when we are standing out in a freezing field trying to get to an elusive feline!

We will continue to offer t-shirts with our Nantucket Cat Rescue logo and to develop projects such as this book to generate funds.

Our continuing objective and commitment is to provide a safe and healthy environment for Nantucket Cats. We will continue to offer educational information about how to care for cats.

The first cats on Nantucket came from the European ships. They served as rodent managers, while keeping the crews and families aboard amused. Some of the ferals are very likely descendants from these early feline visitors, having come ashore at the end of a ship's voyage.

Nantucket Cats are resourceful, independent, adventurous creatures. They are fascinating characters, which, we suppose, would come as no great surprise to the reader, Nantucket being the magical place that we all know and treasure.

So, enjoy the book. Once again, thank you for your support! Happy reading!

Caroline Daniels, Lisa Penn Dias, Cindy Reis Gordon, Margaret Frommer
Nantucket Cat Rescue Founders
P.O. Box 2857, Nantucket, Massachusetts 02584
(508) 825-CATS
(508) 825-2287
July, 2000

Cats are noble,
independent, clean, discrete, dignified,
courageous, and affectionate.
How many of us, I wonder,
are capable of being cats?

The Heart Association
recently reported research that shows
owning a cat can reduce stress,
thereby lowering blood pressure,
and increasing longevity.

Authors and Artists and Cats
"The smallest feline is a masterpiece."
Leonardo da Vinci

Hemingway had 50,
Twain 35; cats have a long literary history.
The first Japanese novel was <u>I Am a Cat</u>, by Soseki
Natsume. Artists, too numerous to mention, have
always loved to paint cats: Antonello da Messina,
Hieronymous Bosch, Jacopo da Ponte Bassano, Paolo
Veronese, Pieter de Hooch, Jan Havicksz Steen, Jean-
Baptiste Simeon Chardin, William Hogarth, Jean-
Baptiste Perroneau,George Stubbs, Francisco Jose de
Goya y Lucientes, Samuel de Wilde, Theodore
Gericault, Ando Hiroshige, John Frederick Lewis,
George Bernard O'Neil, Henriette Ronner-Knip,
Edouard Manet, Louis Eugene Lambert, Horatio Henry
Couldery, Paul Cezanne, Angelo Martinetti, Pierre
Auguste Renoir, Robert Collinson, Sir Lawrence Alma-
Tadema, Ralph Hedley, Theophile Alexandre Steinlen,
Frank Paton, Henri de Toulouse-Lautrec, William
Henry Hamilton, Ada Eliza Tucker, Philip Wilson Steer,
Evelyn de Morgan, John Dickson Batten, Franz Marc,
Louis Wain, Charles van den Eycken, Tsugouharu
(Leonard) Foujita, Henry Tonks, William Gaydon,
Edward Bawden, David Hockney, Ditz,
and Lucy Willis.
What Lovely Company to be in!

Nantucket Cats

by John L. Daniels

Long journeyed Nantucket cats, rationed on rats,
Sailed in on whalers, holed deep under
    canvas sheets,
Jumped ship at Straight Wharf and found
    Pleasant Street
Firesides and sailors' wives who loved them fat,

Or starved or froze or only just sufficed,
Skittering in scrub oak, hurried by hawk eyes.
Hunger drives descendant colonies
Propagating moors, eking out life.

Once feral, and given up for goners,
Shy Molly eventually came around
And princely Jasper proudly struts his ground.
They prove no cats are too wild to honor.

While Polpis house cats lap cream in bliss,
Fogwinded moor cats slink the frozen mist.

Liv

by Loren Brock

My childhood was filled with pets. Many pets.
I spent more time with the cats on my bed, a dog at
my side and creatures in the house and yard than
I spent with people. I learned more about responsibility, companionship and acceptance from my pets
than most people ever learn from other people, and
I learned and loved the most with my cats.

My most enduring friendship with any creature
was with Liv, an Abyssinian mix with a lynx-like
temperament. Liv was nearly full grown when my
sister saved her from the animal shelter. She was
full-grown in the sense that she wasn't going to
grow anymore, there was certainly nothing "full"
about her size. She was a little slip of a thing with a
full-sized personality. She didn't tolerate other cats
and liked humans even less; at first glance (scratch),
I was in love with her. She took a little longer to
warm to me and it was a year before she slept on
my bed. Once she accepted me, however, we spent
the next seventeen years traveling, playing, working
and loving together.

In the years before the odyssey of Liv and me,
most of my pets had stayed close to the house where

I grew up. When I got Liv, I also got gypsy feet, and, by association, she developed gypsy paws. We lived in apartments, rooming houses, cottages and cabins. We got fancy with our gypsy feet and wandered our way into a studio, a loft, a gallery, a yurt, the car, and the Nantucket Lightship.

During our adventures, we weathered a tornado, two hurricanes, several blizzards and a major flood. Liv walked with me on beaches from northern Maine to the southern tip of Florida, hiked half a dozen mountains (on half a dozen feet), and she rode in my backpack by boat, bus, and plane.

Liv and I had a special understanding and trust that did not extend to most. We were Bonnie and Clyde, Christopher Robin and Pooh, Watson and Crick, she was The Claw and I her sidekick. My family and friends thought her fierce, I thought her protective. My husband, who slept with a pillow over his head, found her midnight pouncing frightful and maddening. I found it comforting, knowing we were safe from sneak attack. Safety is in the eye of the beholder.

Liv's beautiful tortoise-shell coat and piercing green eyes belied her fierce temperament and busy claws, and she was at her best and most loving when we traveled in the car. The day I got her we made a seventeen hour trip across country from Michigan to Vermont. For the rest of her life, the car would always be a safe haven for Liv, the swift warm room that saved her from a cold concrete cage in the animal shelter. She rode on a blanket atop the emergency brake or on the seat back, her paws (claws tucked safely away) on my right shoulder, occasionally tapping my face gently, reminding me to stay alert, keep my eyes peeled, put some distance between us and that cold shelter.

I recall one trip from Nantucket to the tip of Florida, fifteen hours of Eastern Seaboard Traffic; Boston, New Haven, the Big Apple with all its in skirts and outskirts (I guess, small apples), New Jersey's chemical corridor, Baltimore, Philly, willy-nilly Washington, stretches of six-lane highway, lit pale green and yellow zooming through fields of former farmland.

Fifteen hours found us finally at the beginning of The South, midday, somewhere temperatures hit one-hundred degrees before noon. Liv (tap, tap, tap) thought we should stop and I agreed. Of course, a little known corollary of an obscure Murphy's law described the situation: on the road, the cost of accommodation, is directly pro-portional to the degree of the traveler's fatigue. Exhausted equals expensive. And, if one is really, really beat, and traveling with a pet, there will be a NO PETS ALLOWED, and the staff will be inordinately suspicious. An hour's search verified that there was exactly ONE room available in the entire metro area - NO PETS, NO EXCEPTIONS, one zillion dollars per night, check out at the crack of dawn.

No problem. Liv and I had been through trickier gigs than this before. Liv was just glad it wasn't an animal shelter. I funneled Liv into the arm of my overcoat, pulled up to the valet parking, set the brake, tossed the keys to the guy in the red hat, draped the coat over my arm (Liv's nose peeking out of the cuff), and marched up to our room like we owned the place. Liv pulled it off like the perfect secret agent -- not a peep, perfectly still, cleverly disguised as a fur coat. The next day, I thought I saw a slight smile from the valet and to this day I'm still not sure if he had us figured the whole time, or he thought I used a litter box when on the road.

As is often the case with vagabonds, spending a lot of time on the road can result in spending many unusual hours off the road, that is; on the side of the road under an overpass in tornado alley watching the sky turn a sickly green, the hail clicking the steamy asphalt, Liv tap-tapping, telling me it's okay, listening to the AM radio guy tersely call county-wide tornado warnings ("...and we have confirmed, well-organized activity on the ground twenty miles south of Terre Haute moving North Northeast at twelve, repeat, on the ground warnings for Charleston, Greencastle, and associated counties, severe damage reported for Centralia and Vadalia, unconfirmed touch downs in the dozens, repeat...")." Liv was slightly ruffled only when I cracked the window to listen for the freight-train roar of a funnel, and, tap, tap, she quickly suggested I roll it up.

Having dodged Dorothy's curse in Indiana, Kentucky and Georgia, Liv and I moved east and experienced New England style weather; colder, more drawn out but certainly more predictable. Snow storms didn't lunge down from the sky at a moment's notice as the lightning and tornadoes had, but once they arrived they stuck around. Liv and I adjusted, although it took some time. We were used to fifteen minutes of terror followed by cautious driving, watching for twisted trees and power lines. Snow storms are slow motion disasters, and as we were used to reacting in minutes, Liv and I tended to be extremely well-prepared by the time snow became a problem.

We became well acquainted with snow and storms our first winters in New England. We may have been slightly over-zealous our first time sliding around in Vermont one November. We were in the backwoods and the snow was deep enough to send my Toyota off the road into a small bank. The jolt flopped Liv, who had been co-piloting on the top of my seat-back as usual, neatly over the steering wheel onto the dash. With the aplomb only agile cats can muster, she stared amused, on the dash with a backdrop of snow, seeming to wag her head slightly back and forth to the rhythm of the wipers, saying, "am I going to have to tap you more often?"

Liv and I were similarly over-prepared for our first hurricane. A hurricane was tracking its way out of the Caribbean and beginning its way North.

The fact that it was traveling at ten to fifteen miles an hour and had hundreds of miles to go if it were to hit Nantucket didn't really register in my tornado brain. Predictable and slow just didn't seem to apply to storms in my mind. At first report (this hurricane was four days away), I bundled Liv into my backpack, strapped her harness on and looped it to my wrist lest we be torn apart by the impending storm. We huddled and fretted for a few hours until friends patiently told me the storm was days away and there would be plenty of time to retreat to high ground. I released Liv to roam my store, the Toy Boat, which she inspected then curled up under the plywood-clad front window as if to say, "Hey, relax."

We were a little more reasonable about the next couple of hurricanes, prepared but no longer reacting knee-jerk to every spinning red blade on the weather channel. Of course, a lowering of the guard coincided with one of the worst storms we've ever had, the "No Name" storm. The Steamship was canceled for days due to sustained winds of seventy miles an hour, the docks were awash with telephone poles, boats and sections of wood piers. The Toy Boat flooded and my car would have floated out to sea if a kind man hadn't lashed it to a telephone pole. Liv and I definitely weren't going to ride this one out in the Toyota. I stashed her in my raincoat as I battened down the hatches and locked the door (looters would have needed scuba gear anyway).

Liv and I weathered the storm in a friend's cottage. I had plenty of time to consider the fact that I had lost my car, most of my belongings and possibly my business. I felt cold and alone and very sad.

Tap, tap, tap. Liv, wet fur sticking out at all angles, to the rescue. She stroked my cheek and licked my face with her tiny rasp of a tongue. It was then I realized no words, however poetic, can aptly express love.

Over the next few years we rebuilt, repaired, repainted (Liv supervised) and bought another car for future trips. Liv stalked the second floor of the store, keeping track of the ferry boats, smacking employees, sleeping on the toys. At night she prowled the first floor like a Doberman, guarding against uninvited toes attached to uninvited burglars. Many nights she would sit immobile in the front window under the spot lights. Passers by would coo and meow. She would give them The Look, a combination of disdain and pity (see how they wish they were cats...). Occasionally, she would do her impression of a stuffed cat, staying so still customers would come by in the morning looking to buy "that beautiful tortoise-shell stuffed kitty." Liv loved to sit on specific piles of books, including, Comet's Nine Lives, and her favorite, Nat, Nat, the Nantucket Cat.

Liv is gone now. She is buried on the hill above my house, surrounded by Iris and Catnip, overlooking Nantucket sunsets. I think of her and miss her every day. Seventeen years is a long time together. They were certainly the very best of times. Friendships like that never really end.

"All right said the cat; and this time it vanished quite slowly, beginning with the end of its tail, and ending with a grin, which remained some time after the rest of it had gone."[1] Tap, tap.

[1]Carroll, Lewis. Alice's Adventures in Wonderland, Great Britain, 1865.

Cats in Our Language

by Jan Jaeger

Cats have been in our history for centuries, sometimes revered and sometimes vilified. The Egyptians are credited with domesticating a species of African wildcat, perhaps as early as 2500 B.C. Worshiped for its role in keeping rodents from the grain stores vital to the Egyptian economy, having a cat in the household was also thought to guarantee many children. In this kitty heyday, the penalty for killing a cat was death. Beloved animals were often mummified and entombed with their owners.

The Egyptians' cats were sacred and their export was forbidden, but they got around nonetheless. Opportunistic and reckless Phoenician sailors managed to smuggle cats into the Middle East and Mediterranean area, selling them for high prices. The Romans are considered responsible for bringing cats to Britain.

In Europe, cats played an important role during the years of the rat-borne Black Plague, in the middle of the 14th century. However, the cat's good reputation was not to last. During the Middle Ages, early European Christians held anything or anyone remotely suggesting a connection with witchcraft as an object upon which to inflict pain and suffering. Perhaps because of its nocturnal habits, cats were thought to be evil. During this time, hundreds of thousands of cats were viciously destroyed.

The Renaissance, spreading to Europe from Italy in the 16th and 17th centuries, fortunately brought good times again to our feline friends. Colonists departing for America brought cats with them to assist in vermin control. Today, happily, the cat is the most popular household pet in this country.

Given the cats' long and varied history, it is interesting to explore the origins of feline-related expressions in our vocabulary. In his book, <u>Catwatching</u>, (Crown Publishers, 1986), author Desmond Morris enlightens us about some of them.

Why is a Male Cat Called a Tom?

This can be traced back precisely to the year 1760 when an anonymous story was published called *The Life and Adventures of a Cat*. In it, the "'ram cat," as a male was then known, was given the name "Tom the Cat." The story enjoyed great popularity, and before long anyone referring to a male cat, instead of calling it a "ram," used the word "Tom," which has survived now for over two hundred years.

Why is a Female Cat Called a Queen?

Because when she is in heat she lords it over the Toms. They must gather around her like a circle of courtiers, must approach her with great deference, and are often punished by her in an autocratic manner.

Why Do We Say "He Let the Cat Out of the Bag"?

The origin of this phrase, meaning "he gave away a secret," dates back to the eighteenth century when it referred to a market-day trick. Piglets were often taken to market in a small sack, or bag, to be sold. The trickster would put a cat in a bag and pretend that it was a pig. If the buyer insisted on seeing it, he would be told that it was too lively to risk opening up the bag, as the animal might escape. If the cat struggled so much that the trickster let the cat out of the bag, his secret was exposed. A popular name for the bag itself was a "poke," hence the other expression, "never buy a pig in a poke."

Why Do We Say "It's Raining Cats and Dogs"?

This phrase became popular several centuries ago at a time when the streets of towns and cities were narrow, filthy and had poor drainage. Unusually heavy storms produced torrential flooding that drowned large numbers of half-starved cats and dogs that foraged there. After a downpour was over, people would emerge from their houses to find the corpses of these unfortunate animals, and the more gullible among them believed that the bodies must have fallen from the sky. Some classicists prefer a more ancient explanation, suggesting that the phrase is derived from the Greek word for a waterfall: *catadupa*. If rain fell in torrents — like a waterfall -- then the saying "raining catadupa," could gradually have been converted into "raining cats and dogs."

Why Do We Say "A Cat Has Nine Lives"?

The cat's resilience and toughness led to the idea that it had more than one life, but the reason for endowing it with nine lives, rather than any other number, has often puzzled people. In ancient times, nine was considered a particularly lucky number because it was a "trinity of trinities" and therefore ideally suited for "lucky" cat.

Now all of you *ailurophiles* (cat lovers) can astound and amaze your friends with these etymological tidbits.

How Cats Came to Nantucket

by Caroline Daniels

The Nantucket Historical Association library is a gold mine of information about life on and around Nantucket. It is located upstairs at the Peter Foulger Museum on Broad Street and is skillfully run by a fleet of staff dedicated to preserving the past for the future. Betsy Lowenstein, Librarian, and Libby Oldham, Research Associate, kindly guided me to the records of animal life on Nantucket.

The first mention of cats came from the journals of men and women who arrived on Nantucket from Europe. They brought cats on board, most often tabby cats, as ratters for the ships. Later, whaling journals describe how cats were brought to Nantucket from various locations, having been picked up along the route, also, for the purpose of ratting.

Some early mentions of animals that lived on the island include rats, snakes, frogs, shrews and moles, rabbits and hares, turtles, seals, deer, mice, birds, including turkeys and hens, owls and hawks, a bullock, hogs, sheep, dogs, pigs, goats, buffaloes, and a hart. Other animals, presumably picked up along the way to amuse the crew or provide sustenance include: a monkey, a parrot, penguins, a terrapin, and an orangutan named, "Doc."

All early mentions of cats are linked with rats. It was the cat's job to reduce the rat population on board ship. Travelers relied on cats ability to rid the ship of rats so that the cargo and provisions would be safe from the rodent's attention. Losing either cargo or provisions had a serious impact on the quality of life of the Captain and his family, when they came along, and, of course, the crew on board. Captain Seabury, sailing by Mariganta Bay, Honolulu in January of 1854, writes about a few tough management issues he had to deal with at the time:

> "regarding smallpox on board contracted by natives but not by white crew. Also 3rd Mate and 8 men stole bow boat and rowed away with all boat sails, iron holepins and other items; also how destructive the rats on board are."[2]

Hopefully, better days were coming for Captain Seabury, but from accounts like this, we can imagine just how important it was to rid the ship of rats. Health, wealth, as well as survival, issues were involved.

---

[2] Business Papers of Charles G. Coffin and Henry Coffin, 1829-1862, Manuscript Collection 152, Folder 164, Edouard A. Stackpole Library and Research Center, Nantucket Historical Association.

Another mention shows the importance of the rat problem in the business of whaling, this from a trip report sent on April 10, 1846 back to the owners of a ship while in Maui by Captain Benjamin C. Sayer, on the voyage of the ship "Edward Carey," 1845-1848:

> "from Benjamin C. Sayer to [owners] relating voyage, loss of runaway, William Har[r]ison, bottom sheathing coming off, smoking ship to rid rats, and mentioning Nantucket ships "Omega," "Levi Starbuck," Henry Brown & _____ Gardner and their oil taken."[3]

Captain Sayer mentions the 3 largest problems, to the crew, the ship, and the cargo and provisions, and then he reported the good news, the oil taken. Rats were serious business.

So, we can understand why a Captain might change the ship's route to find a solution to the rat problem. Here are the words of a sailor from the ship "Peru," in July 18, 1851 off Flores:

> "July 18, 1851 Friday
> Commences with light wind and calm steering L E.
> At night the land bore about N employed on the fore rigging. A steamship passed us bound East. Middle part moderate. At daylight, the weather looked squally. Latter part more wind from the Westward heading in shore and at 8 a.m., the Captain went on shore to get

---

[3] Manuscript Collection 335, Folder 987, Edouard A. Stackpole Library and Research Center, Nantucket Historical Association.

a cat, we having rats on board. Took in the main top gallant sail."[4]

One can only imagine the cat's surprise at one moment walking on land and the next, a heaving ship. Presumably, the cat got on with the job.

The cats also provided amusement and companionship for the sailors and families. The diary of Mary Matilda Taylor is an interesting account of life on board the ship Carolus Magnus, on a voyage from New York to Lima, Peru in 1858. Mrs. Taylor was the wife of Captain Eleazer Taylor. They took their three children along for the entire trip. Her entries describe the enjoyment the family had observing the activities of the cat, Pussy, on board.

"Tuesday, 16th [March, 1858]

Very pleasant today. This morning the rain poured down in torrents on the Deck until quite a pond was formed. Isaac and Jimmy took their shoes off and paddled around in it. The men ran back and forth with their buckets and some were stamping out their clothes on the deck, quite an easy mode of washing. A large school of Dolphins was round the ship today and we were all in hopes one would be caught but were disappointed.

We have got a very cunning Pussy on board the Ship. She walks the deck at night with one of the Mates and tonight we saw her very high up in the Missen rigging.

---

[4] Peru 1851-1855, Manuscript Collection 202, Edouard A. Stackpole Library and Research Center, Nantucket Historical Association.

She is a perfect little sailor. The rain has continued all day and it is quite squally most of the time."[5]

Watching a cat navigate the rigging must have amused the children and provided comic relief to the routine of sea life.

After a grueling time rounding Cape Horn, the family was eager to head for port, which they did a few weeks later. Pussy provided the sign that the ship was nearing land:

"Friday, April 16th, 1858

Weather continues unsettled. A heavy sea rolling so that I can scarcely write. I feel very well today. Pussy caught a bird last night. We found the wings on the deck this morning. We all begin to feel very anxious to get in port as we have had a pretty long passage thus far, or at least since we came in the neighborhood of Cape Horn."

Their voyage continued with much more pleasant weather.

Cats, not indigenous to Nantucket, were brought here mainly from Europe, but also from many points the whaling ships passed, the four corners of the globe. Having finished their job on board, they were released on Nantucket. Some were kept as household pets while others were set loose to fend for themselves. Many of today's feral cats are most probably descendants of the early shipboard cats.

---

[5] Morris Family Papers/Brown Collection, 1802-1908, Manuscript Collection 250, Edouard A. Stackpole Library and Research Center, Nantucket Historical Association. Special thanks to Mary Ayer for donating the diary to the Nantucket Historical Association.

© 1999 N. Caroline Daniels

Pickles

by Danielle Frommer

Pickles was a sleek black cat, who lived to the great age of 24 years. For all but the last two years of his life, he lived on Straight Wharf. He warmed himself, standing with elegance in the sun, against the old Artists' Association building when it was located on Straight Wharf. He wandered over to the A & P, where the employees often fed him and admired his grace. He had an innate dignity and graciously accepted food from many kind friends.

He was street-wise, and was able to survive Nantucket winters by taking advantage of reflected sunlight on plate glass windows. He sought and found the pockets of warmth in town. He had various cubby holes to hunker down in.

During the twenty-second year of his life, Nantucket was blasted by sub-zero weather and I knew Pickles couldn't survive this winter without help. Against the advice of many, who thought Pickles would not stay in a house, I brought him home.

He took to the luxury of an electric blanket on a luxuriously soft mattress as to the manor born.

After all, he had royal Siamese bloodlines, which one could see from his high cheekbones and regal bearing.

He spent his final two years in my home as a pampered, much loved, house cat.

© 1999 N. Caroline Daniels

Momma Cat and BB

by Nancy Simonton

This is the story of Momma Cat and BB and how they came to live with me. It is also the story of a close bond between his Mother cat and her son, and a happy ending to what could have been another tragic, neglected animal story.

I first saw Momma Cat in April 1996, as she purposefully headed for the stairs in "THE NANTUCKET BEACON" office. I followed the little calico down and watched as everyone greeted her, petted her, then fed her bits of bread, cheese, and sandwich meat. She had pale green eyes, a white "bib" and stomach. Her paws were white but her front paws looked like baseball mitts due to an extra toe on each, like the famous Hemingway cats. She was sweet and very skilled at getting handouts and an ear scratch, using those big front paws to tap people on the leg for attention.

When I asked about her, the staff told me she belonged to a neighbor but came to eat lunch at the BEACON every day. I mentioned she was probably hungry due to being pregnant, but everyone insisted that she had been spayed. They told me she'd had a litter several months before and her owner had promised to get her "fixed." The staff had found homes for the kittens and asked the owner to take care of the operation. Still sure she was expecting, I set up cat food and water for her.

At the end of May, I came to work on a Monday morning to find Momma Cat sitting on the steps of "THE BEACON," waiting patiently for the first arrival. She ran in, headed for the cat food, ate the lot, and ran out. I followed and saw her scoot under the steps, peeked and saw her with three kittens. She was trying to keep them warm on the cold ground, so we shoved old coats and towels under the steps for her. Momma Cat and her babies snuggled in promptly. We put food and water for her under the steps too, and I came in over the weekend to be sure she was okay.

The next week continued chilly and drizzly, and one day Momma came in and prowled around the whole office. I was sure she was looking for a warm, dry, safe place for her babies. Sure enough, she began bringing them in one by one and carry-ing them downstairs. The biggest one, a striped kitten, howled the whole way down. She hid them between a long credenza and a wall, barely enough room for her to squeeze through, but not big enough for any of us to bother her. We set up a litter box inside, food bowls, etc. Momma seemed voracious, which we attributed at the time to nursing three kittens.

The first time I really saw BB, the howling striped cat, was when he made his first venture out of the nursery. He was twice as big as his siblings, and I promptly named him Buster (later amended to BB for Bad Boy). The other two, a calico and a tabby, females, eventually wandered out to meet everyone. BB was the most confident, socialized cat I'd ever seen. Momma taught him how to beg for handouts in an endearing way and he freely gave affection to everyone. He also had no qualms about walking all over his sisters to get food or attention. Inquisitive and rambunctious, he was often causing mayhem of some kind. As he grew, his hair became longer and fuller and his tail was spectacular and ringed. BB had Momma's white bib and feet though, and tawny yellow eyes.

Everyone at "THE BEACON" was already fond of Momma and loved the kittens. They got lots of attention, but Momma was the most attentive of all to her offspring. She was a great Mother, keeping track of them always, calling them when she could not locate one of them. When they were about two months old, she even brought in a dead mouse, called them, and gave a demonstration on how to bat it around. Presumably this was to prepare them for life by showing them how to catch one themselves.

Flea dipping was done when the kittens were three months old and no longer nursing. We had Momma and the kittens treated for worms, which had been another reason Momma had been so hungry, eaten so much, yet stayed so thin.

We learned that Momma's owner probably had a serious drug problem and was in danger of being evicted. Momma was with us and her kittens around the clock, so we decided to take full responsibility for her and her family. Her two female kittens left at three months to live with a reporter and are still there and very contented with their home together.

Momma did not seem to miss them but was very anxious when she could not find BB anywhere, crying piteously while searching the office for him. I began to worry about what would happen when I took BB home and momma continued to live in the office. My husband had met and fallen in love with BB, but we already had one cat, and he thought three would be too many in our small house.

After the girls left and Momma definitely was not nursing anymore, we took up an office collection to get her shots and spayed. I took BB and Momma to the MSPCA for shots, left her for surgery and took him home. The MSPCA workers said BB was definitely sired by a Maine Coon Cat, they had treated two other kittens in the vicinity of "THE BEACON" who looked like him.

Momma came to our house after her surgery to recuperate. She was supposed to go back to "THE BEACON" after she felt better, but that is not the way it worked out. She stayed in a room by herself the first night to rest. Bright and early the following morning, BB was standing at the door to her room, crying, and I could hear her answering. I let BB in and they had a spectacular reunion, licking each other and purring loudly. Clearly, they loved being together and had missed each other. My husband was touched by this and decided three cats would not be so hard.

We live in Maine now and Momma and BB are still with us. She still loves cheese and bread and still asks for them by taps with those baseball mitt paws, but she is heavier and healthier now. Momma is an affectionate cat and friendly to most visitors to the house. BB has matured into a huge, handsome cat and he is clearly the king of the castle. He charms everyone he meets, maintains his dignity most of the time, but still has bursts of orneriness. When he wants something, he does not take no for an answer.

Our house is much larger than our Nantucket home and the cats scatter all over. Momma and BB each have their own schedules, exercising their independent feline attitudes. Yet, there are times when Momma cannot find BB and will walk through our house calling until he answers her or runs to see her.

Just this morning, BB was sunning in an upstairs bedroom window when Momma began crying as she searched for him downstairs. His ears went up and he looked in the direction of her call. A moment later, he jumped down and ran downstairs to greet her. Their reunion was as affectionate as always, with much licking and purring. All was well again in Momma's world.

Willie, Cat about Town

by Caroline Daniels

Willie, perhaps one of the best loved, certainly better known cats on the island, was a cat about town. He visited a number of restaurants, shops, and entertainment spots, changing his routine the way a socialite might, with the changing seasons, hitting all of the high interest places, at just the right time. He was social, yet independent. He liked what he liked, went where he wanted to go, and, if you liked it, fine; if not, he didn't give a fig. Willie was his own cat. He was a handsome tabby cat, with attitude.

When Debby Fraker, of the Lion's Paw on Main Street, talks about him, her head goes back, she smiles, and there is a certain mist around her eyes.

"Every day he would wait at the step at the Lion's Paw. He had his routine. We kept the food in here." She pointed to a cupboard. "We would have dry food in here, his staple food. If we had run out, he would sit right on the counter until we had gone to the A&P, and returned with the food. Then, he would go for a nice sleep on one of the beds in the back rooms."

The Lion's Paw sells furniture, gifts, china, a whole assortment of quality goods. Dan Bills, the owner, laughs, "He liked to follow the sun in the shop, and sleep in the best spots. This would be on a bed or a sofa, always on a *choice* piece of furniture. He especially appreciated the mohair, the throws."

"We always kept food, and little treats for him. Customers loved Willie. He would sit in the windows, largely in command. Visitors would look for Willie from season to season. As things were sold or replaced, he'd adjust, look for the next new wonderful piece of furniture and claim it.

"He would sit in the front window watching the passersby, and when he'd had enough people watching, or he'd had enough of people cat watching, he would hide under one of the tables.

"He had his routine. Of course, he had different quarters in the Winter. Sometimes he would ride around on the front seat in one of the cabs all night. They would all give him rides.

"He attended lectures at the Atheneum, the creche at the Catholic Church, the film theaters, the art galleries. He went to several restaurants.

"There used to be a shop on Straight Wharf that draped fabric over the rafters in swoops to decorate the ceiling. One day I walked in and the owner pointed to a particular sagging spot in one of the drapes, of course, it was Willie."

Debby Fraker described one long visit Willie made in the winter, "It was Christmas Eve and I had left a present behind in the shop because I had wanted it to be a surprise. I came down to get it very late, and there, on the step, was Willie."

"I said, oh Willie, you can't come in tonight, no one will be here tomorrow, we're closed for awhile. He just looked at me. I went to get my package, and when I came out, he was sitting by my car."

"I said, do you want to come in? Well, he got in. He came to my home for about ten days. He went in, he went out. My dog and my cat just let him, and the dog is a Jack Russell! They don't just accept new cats like that! Willie had an air about him, and they didn't bother him at all.

"It was as if he had come home with me for a little vacation, a little R&R. Then one day, he just looked at me, as if to say, 'Thanks, I'll be going now.' And, he went out, walking from my home near the windmill down to town again."

Willie was born in Vermont and was brought to Nantucket in 1989 by Peter Reitzas, a weaver at Nantucket Looms. Peter would bring Willie with him to work. While he sat upstairs weaving, he opened a window which led to a system of roof lines that enabled Willie to wander. And, that was the beginning of Willie's taste for town.

Soon Willie had found the best food and warmth spots and set up something of a routine. He had two, at least two, places that would provide the staples of his diet dry food and treats: Nantucket Looms and the Lion's Paw. Then, he would move on to restaurants that included, and this may not be a complete list: the Ropewalk, Straight Wharf Restaurant, the Club Car, the Tavern, Arno's, and Congdon's Pharmacy. When scallops were in season, he would saunter down to the scalloping shanty, where they would feed him until he could eat no more, whereupon he would climb the ladder to the loft and sleep off the excesses.

Peter Reitzas had left his Visa card number with the MSPCA to take care of any health care costs, but Willie had his numerous supporters when it came to care too. Occasionally, he would move into someone's home for a time. He stayed with Brooks and Elizabeth Wynn for two years, then he'd be off again, always returning to town.

Willie lived life the way he wanted to live it. As Liz Winship, from Nantucket Looms, said, "It was nice that he was around. He was happy and independent. People appreciated him. He was very good at taking care of himself. He had a good life."

Willie acted ill the last few days of his life. True to form, he tried to tend to his illness alone. He was found by Debby Fraker just outside the Lion's Paw. There is a rumor that he was hit by a car, but those who saw him do not believe that. There were no cuts or abrasions, just a calm expression on his face.

There is a cobblestone in the sidewalk, just by the streetlight, in front of Nantucket Looms, with

"Willie" written, as a tribute. Willie, the Nantucket town cat, lived life as he wanted and will always be loved by all.

Prodigal Kitty

by Jan Jaeger

My planned topic for this week went out the window when our prodigal kitty, Jezebel, namesake of another biblical troublemaker, came home this rainy Sunday. This trip away was exceptionally long, and I was beginning to mentally steel myself for the final acceptance of her never returning. Unpleasant images of an injured or dead cat kept popping up in my head. Plaguing me were increasing worry and self-condemnation about being an irresponsible pet owner by allowing our cats freedom, and questioning the wisdom of that decision.

Now, as Jezebel contentedly power-napped on an afghan Fred's Mother crocheted for us many years ago, I know she has been living the life of a true cat, and I wish she could share with me where she has spent the past several weeks. She is a little thinner but otherwise appears unscathed, still wearing her collar and a faded name tag. I am grateful to the inclement weather if that is what has finally urged her to return. In her sleep, she occasionally voices a plaintive and lonesome howl, perhaps dreaming of a perilous encounter or particularly harrowing experience, or maybe just subliminally testing to see if she has company in the house, as I instinctively respond to her call. Happily, I phone the MSPCA to remove her name from their missing list.

We adopted Jezebel from the Humane Society in Greeley, Colorado, over eleven years ago, when she was the teeniest kitten imaginable, a jet-black stray. She always was a very silent kitty, rarely vocalizing; even today, her purrs must be felt rather than heard. If she inadvertently got herself into a closet or cupboard, the search to locate her would become frantic because she would never help by answering our calls. In those days, she seemed to enjoy her infrequent trips outside, seizing the rare opportunity to climb up on the roof or up into our huge pine trees. Our weekend travels into the back country of Colorado in a small recreational vehicle, acquired specifically for the purpose of taking our pets along, was an adventure. Jezebel would accompany us on walks with Geronimo, while timid Jetti clung to the familiar campsite, usually hiding under the RV. Perhaps this is where the wanderlust began.

Otherwise, our two cats were kept inside for safety and security. After moving to our present home, we discovered that our dirt road was quiet and untraveled except by those living there, with several of our neighbors elsewhere off season. So, we decided to install cat doors. In fact, this is how we gained our third cat, Miz Edna, who was wise in the ways of cat doors and knew what went out also went in. All three cats use the doors at will, but Jezebel is the only one who wanders. The other two stay close by, eager to greet us when we arrive home, happy to sit with us outside on the deck and always ready to curl up in a favorite spot in the house to sleep.

We have speculated that Jezebel has selected an alternate summer home, perhaps one offering canned food or the crunchy, junky stuff, or that she hangs out with a feral colony to express her wild side, but we consider these scenarios improbable. More likely, as an avid hunter, she lives off the land, foraging from the abundant supply of wildlife and finding cozy hideouts for sleeping. If, as I have read, the typical meal of cat food is the equivalent of five mice, she has had a formidable provisioning job.

A couple of summers ago, when Jezebel was on another "walk-about," by chance I flipped to Channel 3 for a few minutes. The MSPCA was running an ad for animals at the shelter. Described was a young, black cat found in the Dionis area. I immediately thought of our missing Jezebel and gave them a call. When I was told that this cat, fitting the description of my own except for the age, had been adopted, the MSPCA was good enough to share the name of a distant neighbor who was the rescuer. And my neighbor was then good enough to allow me to visit her newly acquired cat. Imagine my chagrin to discover that this was, in fact, Jezebel. My neighbor graciously surrendered this wandering pet to its guilty Mother.

Short of keeping all three confined, we have had to come to terms with the fact that periodically, Jezebel leaves home. We have had difficulty adjusting to her absences, and over time we have had to recognize that her need to take a "walk-about" apparently will not change. And so we respect her choices, wait for her appearances, and trust in her innate homing ability to bring her safely back. And, like the prodigal son, she will be joyfully welcomed and feted when she chooses to grace us with her beautiful presence.

Strays are kept at the Nantucket MSPCA for one week to give the owners a chance to claim them. After one week, the animals are put up for adoption in the shelter. So, please give your animals identification tags with safety collars! And, call the Nantucket MSPCA if your animal is missing!

It's George, by George!

by Mary Miles

George was indeed gorgeous. He was a hefty cat, a significant cat, an independent and self-assured cat. Not smooth and sophisticated, not suave and urbane, but a cat possessing a definite presence just this side of charisma. He wasn't exactly patronizing, but he had that feline talent of occasionally sitting with his back to you, ears bent slightly downward, in unmistakable disapproval just *that* side of disdain.

As a mature male, he was a bruiser — almost 23 pounds surrounded by an impressive, well-groomed orange fur coat. And how did it happen that he became something of a Sumo? Just ask anyone at the Nantucket MSPCA.

It happened this way.

As an adorable little marmalade kitten, he was skittery and playful, but fate intervened and dealt George a mean blow, in the form of a door closed too firmly and a tail that, you might say, didn't quite pull through. Yes, this small creature had his tail caught in a door, an accident that remains at least Number 3 on a Mama Cat's list of things for infant kitties to avoid.

As a result of that disaster, the unfortunate feline found himself at the MSPCA, where the caring, support, and attention he received quite convinced him that he would pull through and that this was definitely a place that deserved to be graced by his continual presence. He became the "house cat." George greeted all incoming human creatures and their pets — including dogs, which, naturally, worried him not in the slightest. He was born with that kind of savoir-faire, after all.

Following a fair amount of time — six years, in fact — during which George enjoyed affection, attention, and a certain fame at the MSPCA, he got to feeling perhaps a bit big for his boots, occasionally nipping the hand that reached to pat him. The fame was in danger of becoming notoriety. That wouldn't do, not at all. Consequently, the staff, unwilling to dismiss him altogether from his position as charge-d'affaires, put him into a closed back room when the front doors opened for business. It was a room, mind you, not a cell. It goes without saying that George did not consider this any sort of exile or punishment; having a healthy ego, he undoubtedly reasoned that he'd been promoted. The cat cages were in that room, and he kept the temporarily resident cats in line and apprised of goings-on in the larger world. Yes, George seemed to have settled into his altered status peaceably and benignly.

Aha, thought the MSPCA staff members, we did

the right thing and didn't traumatize this beloved orange cat. All was hunky-dory, they thought, congratulating themselves on their strategy.

But... it happens that atop those cat cages were kept huge bags of cat food, ready for purchase. Alas and alack — ultimately the folly of placing George in a space filled with food became apparent. However, for a happy, heady time, George would arise every morning, give himself a thorough cleaning, then select his meal of the moment. Will it be turkey today? Ah, perhaps the veal... Tuna for Sunday dinner.

The 18 claws of this orange critter (yes, 18, not 20 — count 'em on any cat and see) were impressive. With dispatch, elan, and a distinct air of noblesse oblige, George carefully opened up slits in most of the bags — just big enough to withdraw and devour his daily allowance...and them some. In fact, and then *a lot*.

George grew and grew. He never fought — he didn't have to...to have challenged ever-larger George would have been foolhardy indeed. From ambling to waddling, almost, went George until one day a staff member pulled down a huge bag of cat food. Then, and only then, was the disaster perceived in full and awful bloom. Bag after bag, the hapless humans discovered, leaked food. Dribbling tidbits, then a steady flow, finally a virtual cascade of healthy little kibbles, falling all over the place.

Oh, *George!*

Well, plainly, this big gent had to go. But who would take the extremely full-grown cat? Even with real concerns on the part of the MSPCA staff, all was soon well, in spite of his size and now not-so-dazzling reputation.

George was taken in by Loren and Gavin...or maybe that should be expressed the other way around. There were already several cats on the premises, so Gavin, a wonderful and magical artist with wood, and despite being basically a dog person, agreed not only to take George into his domain to become Official Workshop Cat, but he apparently gave the sizable fellow leave to command the dogs, sort of, from a wonderful set of platforms...one level for sleeping, one for eating (his favorite occupation) and gazing down at his kingdom of workers and dogs, one for climbing out the window to go outdoors.

George would go out rantum-scooting, meandering who knows where, checking out his properties and friends, pleasantly reminding the wildlife of his important presence, and would come back in a day, or two, or maybe even three. But he always came back. For three years he ruled successfully over his domains. Then, in May of 2000, he went out and didn't come back. Because he occasionally returned to the MSPCA to visit, Loren and Gavin didn't worry too much at first - they'd assumed he'd gone on another of his little vacations. Then the MSPCA called. He was gone; someone had found him, ill, along the road. He had, it seems, a great heart that finally gave out on him. But everyone who ever knew George remembers him fondly.

"He was an interesting combination of ornery and amiable," said Loren. "He was formidable...but I must say he never nipped me. He was a great cat, a sort of man about town. While we had George, the mouse population went way down, and because of that, so did the tick count. He wasn't afraid of the biggest, barkiest dog. We will always love George."

Surely, George, the forever 9-year-old, orange, twenty-three pound cat, is somewhere taking charge. He was certainly one of Nantucket's most interesting and well-known cats. Wherever he is, we wish him well.

Cookie

by Lisa Penn Dias

I had successfully trapped two feral kittens in September of 1997. They had been living underneath our front porch since their Mother moved them there in an attempt to give them shelter from the sometimes stormy, September weather that Nantucketers understand all too well.

They appeared to be healthy, and were definitely active little fuzz balls, playing amongst the rose bushes, and shrubs in the sunshine, chasing each other's tail and pouncing the rose petals that flittered in the grass each time a breeze came up.

They had no curiosity about humans though. If my husband or I walked outside onto the porch, they would vanish in a matter of seconds. The only interest that they took in us was from a distance. Occasionally, at night, and always first thing in the morning, they would sit on the back of the chair on the porch and peer into our bedroom window. It seemed like they wanted to see what life was like "on the inside."

Once they were old enough to be taken from their Mother, I began to want to take them under my wing and tame them, but one of our house cats at the time required special care. I felt the best situation for the kittens would be to take them to Nantucket's MSPCA. I met with Barbara, the head of the shelter, to ask her to please let me know if she had difficulty in taming or placing them. I would figure out some way to assist. I gave her a donation toward their care, said goodbye, and left.

Five weeks later, I received a phone call at work. It was Barbara. She had kept her promise and she had remembered mine.

"The kittens that you surrendered to us were difficult to tame," she said. My heart sank. "The little golden tabby came around and was adopted last week." My heart rate became a little more regular. "The black one...well, ...he's just not coming around. We've had him here for five weeks, Lisa, and he's still hissing and swatting at people. No one wants a hissing kitten."

There was a moment of silence. Then, she went on to say, "I truly believe that if he were in a home environment, he would come around, and I really want him to have the chance." My spirits brightened!

With that I quickly asked what our time frame was for Cookie's fate. I had a week to find a foster home. My friend Mark said he would take him, but he was leaving on vacation for a week.

"Phew," I thought, "Cookie now has a place to go."

I called Barbara and gave her the good news.

I was off from work the next day, so I went to the shelter to see if I could make any headway with the reluctant kitten, now 4 months old. Cookie was in the corner of the cage. I spoke softly to him for a while. It seemed that I was not getting anywhere.

I asked Barbara for a towel so that I could attempt to pick him up and protect myself at the same time. After about five minutes or so, Cookie started kneading my towel-protected arm with his two front paws, "making biscuits," as my sister says.

"Progress," I thought.

I continually stroked his jet-black fur — he seemed to like it. I asked permission to use the animal control office to place him on the floor to try to coax him into playing with me. It worked!

Still scared and skeptical, Cookie would hide under the chair for what seemed like hours. After about two hours, I said, "I'll take him to our house for the next week...waiting another week here for his foster home would only delay his chance of being tamed."

We were pushing the envelope already. Usually, after 16 weeks, it is very difficult to tame a feral/wild kitten.[6]

So, off we went! We walked in the front door and were greeted by three of our house cats. They

---

[6] Editorial Note: We are learning more all of the time about how to socialize feral kittens and cats. We have successfully tamed kittens and cats of all ages. It must be pointed out, however, that the earlier a kitten is exposed to petting and playing with a human, the easier it is to socialize.

sniffed the kennel, turned on their paws and walked away as if to say, "another one."

I placed the kennel in our guest room. I left Cookie in it while I gathered the necessary supplies: litter box, food, and water bowls, rolled up balls of aluminum foil, which make an easy cat toy, fur mice and a comfy blanket for a bed.

Having gathered all of the supplies, I closed the door with Cookie and me, alone in his new room. I opened the kennel. He immediately leapt out and ran to hide underneath an upholstered chair.

Whenever I entered the room for the next two days, he reacted the same way. On the third day, I grabbed a pillow and lay on the floor next to the chair peering under the chair at Cookie. I told myself that this was to be the day for progress — I was not leaving until I could get some positive response from him.

I stretched my arm out under the chair and spoke to him softly. I literally told him, "Cookie, your days are numbered, knowing that an outdoor feral cat usually lives a few years, whereas a house cat can live up to twenty or more years. Please let me help you."

Right after that, he began to rub the back of his neck on the underside of the chair. A few minutes later, he let out the most beautiful, sweet, "Meeeeeowwwww," and quickly approached my face (remember I am laying on the floor with the left half of my upper body squashed under the chair).

It all happened so quickly. It was a moment that I will never forget. He pushed his little face right into mine, purring and licking all the while! WOW!

I continued to work with him for the next two weeks. I introduced him to other people, played with him, and gave him unconditional love and attention. Once he was properly socialized, I called Barbara and told her that he was ready for a good home. She had a young woman that was looking for a kitty, so we made a date for her to come to our home and meet Cookie. She loved him and went to see Barbara to fill out the necessary paperwork.

Isn't that a great story?

What's Your Cat's Sign?

by Jan Jaeger

For centuries, people have believed cosmic forces influence life experiences, shape personalities and predetermine destinies. Should animals be any less subject to the heavenly auras than their owners? Reprinted and adapted from a publication of the Humane Society of Weld County, Colorado, these sun sign descriptions apply to the feline kingdom. If you know your cat's birthday, perhaps the character traits listed here are no surprise.

AQUARIUS: The Water Bearer (*January 21 - February 18*)
The Aquarius cat is inventive, intelligent, unpredictable, decorative and rather aloof. Inquisitive, this cat rarely displays affection for humans, preferring to observe from afar.

PISCES: The Fish (*February 19 - March 20*)
The Pisces cat is sensitive and big-hearted. Home is where his/her heart is. Attention centers on their owners, who can be assured of single-minded devotion.

ARIES: The Ram *(March 21 - April 20)*
Adventurous creatures, Aries cats are natural leaders. Although fiercely independent, they have a very loyal streak and adore being fussed over when in the right mood.

TAURUS: The Bull *(April 21 - May 21)*
The Taurean cat is always purring and is happiest when asleep on its favorite bed. They love food and not surprisingly, tend to be rather plump, placid and easy-going.

GEMINI: The Twins *(May 22 - June 21)*
A restless cat not well suited to be a constant, lap-loving companion. An incurable flirt, this cat's lively nature makes for fascinating, sometimes exasperating, company.

CANCER: The Crab *(June 22 - July 22)*
Ideal for someone at home a lot, the Cancer cat is constantly at your side and into your lap at every opportunity. But treat carefully, these cats are easily offended.

LEO: The Lion *(July 23 - August 22)*
Leo cats must rule the roost unchallenged. They have a striking appearance and keep their coats in shape. They adore praise and will go out of their way to attract attention.

VIRGO: The Virgin *(August 23-September 22)*
"Take no risks" is this cat's motto. Intelligent

thinkers, Virgo cats don't mind if their owner is out all day but love a change of scene. This cat is tranquil, never in a bad mood.

LIBRA: The Scales *(September 23 - October 22)*
You can't pamper this sensuous feline too much. Librans crave attention, are quick to take offense and don't take kindly to being unceremoniously shooed off a comfy chair.

SCORPIO: The Scorpion *(October 23 - November 22)*
Passionate, magical cats with magnetic presence. Energetic and loving life, this cat is slow to make friends, but once won over, will be your trusty ally for life.

SAGITTARIUS: The Archer *(November 23 - December 21)*
Freedom-loving rovers, Sagittarian cats lack the grace of other signs. Their great interests in life are eating and human company, but too much fuss makes them impatient.

CAPRICORN: The Goat *(December 22 - January 21)*
Unruffled and serene, Capricorn cats are rather timid with strangers. They crave affection but may feel inhibited about demanding it, so a sensitive owner is helpful.

Insights into your cat's predispositions and attributes can add another element into understanding behaviors of your present cats or to predicting future compatibility. Just ask your cat, "What's your sign?"

Sammy Tucker, A Dog of a Cat

by Lynn Tucker

I'd always heard that cats come into your life if you're lucky enough to be on their path. Well, I wasn't expecting this little gray character to enter my heart and life. During a very sad time in my life, when I needed a bit of luck, this little kitten did just that.

My sweet 13 year old golden retriever Nickolaus was terribly sick with cancer. On one particular day during our visit to the MSPCA, a young man walked in holding a gray kitten gently on his shoulder.

For a second, I exchanged a sense and knowing and an energy from this kitten's eyes. Suddenly, I blurted out, "I've got to have that kitten!"

The ladies at the front desk of the MSPCA knew a bond when they saw one and nodded in agreement.

The kitten came home with Nickolaus and me that day and adjusted naturally. Playful with me, he was also gentle and loving to Nickolaus. It was as though the kitten was meant to be with us. I named him Sammy, a nickname I had for my Nana.

Nickolaus's cancer advanced slowly but the inevitable time came when he passed away. I lay on my bed thinking of all of the wonderful times we had together, but soon tears welled up and spilled down my cheeks.

I felt a soft tap on my shoulder. Sammy crawled around and sat on my chest. He came up to my face, looked me in the eyes and started wiping my tears with his tiny paws. I can still recall the tenderness on my face.

From that day on, Sammy took on a lot of the characteristics I normally associate with a dog. He drives in the car, accompanies me on walks and curls up with friends when they visit. Since I haven't had a cat for many years, I treat him like a dog and carry on the activities I had shared with Nickolaus, with Sammy. He loves bottle corks which he retrieves and drops at my feet. He sits for treats, but somehow he never quite managed paw shaking.

Sammy has been with me for many happy years, one of the happiest characters in my life. I have always been grateful for his love.

Rules Our Cats Live By

by Jan Jaeger

Anyone who has pets knows that as owners we are the alpha or dominate pack member. It can become quickly apparent, though, that we don't always have the upper hand. I thought it would be fun this week to take a lighthearted look at some rules any of us with pets can relate to. The source of this piece is, unfortunately, anonymous.

Basic Rules for Cats Who Have a House to Run:

1. CHAIRS AND RUGS: If you have to throw up, get into a chair quickly. If you cannot manage in time, get to an Oriental rug. If there is no Oriental rug, shag is good.

2. DOORS: Do not allow closed doors in any room. To get a door opened, stand on your hind legs and hammer with your forepaws. Once this door is opened, it is not necessary to use it. After you have ordered an outside door opened, stand halfway in and halfway out and think about several things. This is particularly important during very cold weather, rain, snow, and the mosquito season.

3. GUESTS: Quickly determine which guest hates cats the most. Sit on that lap. If you can arrange to have fish breath, so much the better. For lap-sitting or rubbing against trouser legs, select a fabric color which contrasts with your fur. For example, white cats should choose black wool clothing and vice-versa. For a guest who claims to love cats, be prepared with aloof disdain to apply claws to stockings and use a quick nip on the ankle.

4. TABLE-WALKING: When walking among dishes on the table, be prepared to look surprised and hurt if scolded. The idea to convey is, "but you allow me on the table when company is not here."

5. BATHROOM ETIQUETTE: Always accompany guests to the bathroom. It is not necessary to do anything but sit and stare.

6. COOKING: When supervising cooking, sit just behind the left heel of the cook. You thereby have a better chance of being stepped on and picked up and consoled.

7. WORK ETHIC: If one of your humans is sewing or writing and another is idle, stay with the busy one. For knitting projects, curl quietly into the lap of the knitter and pretend to doze. Occasionally reach out and slap the knitting needles. The knitter may try to distract you with a scrap of yarn. Ignore it! The idea is to hamper work. When your human is reading, get in close

under the chin between the eyes and the book unless you can lie across the book itself.

8. PLAY: Remember to get lots of sleep during the day, so that you are fresh for playing cat and mouse or king of the hill on your human's head between 2 and 4 a.m.

9. TRAINING: It is important to begin people training early. Humans need to be taught the basic rules. If you start early and are consistent, they can be taught and you can have a smoothly running household in no time.

10. AFFECTION: Let the human know how much you want to be stroked by rubbing, purring, and acting coquettish. Roll over on your back and squint your eyes. When the human starts to touch your tummy which is so invitingly displayed, nail them, preferably with all four feet. Extra points for teeth too!

Her Royal Highness, Thistle

by Mary Miles

She is a very special cat, and was from the very beginning. I'd had two male Siamese in the past, her half- brothers, it turned out, and now I was ready for a new kitty. So, I contacted the breeder,[7] and yes, she said she had about six females who were pregnant. The only hitch: this woman (who lived on Black Cat Road!) was about to have hip surgery, so all the cats, male and female, were about to be transported to the home of her daughter. Did I want to "contract" for a young female anyhow? Yes!

I knew that Siamese were a different kind of critter; the Father will not only tolerate the kittens, he will groom them and care for them in the box when the Mother is absent, looking somewhat quizzical when the babies root fruitlessly for the source of their ongoing meal. My kids owned a neutered lilac-point male Siamese decades ago at the same time our wee dachshund gave birth to puppies, eight of them (too many for her, so we all had to bottle-feed the babies). "Sphinx" benevolently

---

[7] Nantucket Cat Rescue suggests that those who are looking to share their lives with a cat should look in the animal shelters...millions of cats and kittens are killed each year because of overpopulation.

offered his warm, furry body to the adorable puppy kids when Chloe was taking a rest from her chores as a brand-new Mom. Same look of confusion when the pups, to my children's delight, looked persistently for the spigots. But Sphinx was game and he cleaned and babysat very efficiently.

When the time of birthing of the new cats came around, in March of 1991, I received a call saying that yes, the kittens had all been born — more than 20 of them. But tragedy: apparently confused by the change of location, the new mamas didn't adequately feed or care for their babies, and they had died — all but one, a female chocolate-point. Would I like her if she survived? YES! I waited anxiously for five weeks and sure enough, this tough little lady, who to this day believes wholeheartedly that not only is she a tiger but she rules the entire world, was still alive and doing very well.

The first thing I did was to rule out distemper or other feline ailments with my friendly Vet. This cat was fine. I named her Thistle, because her eyes were a clear, magical bluish-violet...and her claws were like tiny curved scimitars! She greeted me anywhere by hopping onto the bottom of my jeans and climbing quickly upward, to my shoulder. (At first she wanted to perch on the top of my head like some sort of furry canary, but I discouraged that, and to this day she likes to drape herself around my back and shoulders like a moving mink, whenever we go anywhere.)

A white, skinny creature whose back legs seemed longer than the front ones and whose huge ears were entirely disproportionate to the rest of her, Thistle immediately owned me, my apartment, and everything in it.

Drapes, mantels, dressers, computer, lamps, and refrigerator — everything was her Everest to conquer. I squirted her with a water pistol when she got onto the stove and dining table, and when she decided scaling the screens was more fun than a barrel of mice. One of my sons, now grown, said I shouldn't have done that last, however, saying that he routinely clipped the long claws of his fierce little ex-feral cat while his wife scooted her up onto the screen door, holding her there just long enough so that Stephen, on the other side, could handily trim the barbs sticking out. Painless and even fun for the cat.

As she began to acquire a beautiful beige coat, her facial mask, paws, ears, and tail began darkening dramatically, yet Thistle lost none of her joie de vivre. I meant for her to be an inside cat after utterly failing to get her accommodated to a small leash just for porch outings. She'd flip and somersault and ultimately get herself thoroughly tangled, and was so persistent in refusing to wear halter and leash, that I gave up. The price of that adventure was her lifelong commitment to GETTING OUTSIDE at all costs, and employing the swiftest, cleverest ruses to do so. She's escaped a few times briefly, throwing me into anxious hysteria. If you think a grown woman doesn't feel peculiar *eraing-ing* and *erowrrring* all up and down the streets of the neighborhood, you're wrong. She will come if you whistle or imitate her piercing call (not *meow*), but never to the traditional, "Here, kitty, kitty," accompanied by that lips-pursed squeak most cats attend to.

What more can I say about my best friend? So much! But, to make it succinct, here's a list:

• She became a national traveler at age 1, when she drove to California and back with me one Spring.

• She adores the warm top of a computer and will gently knock off any little gizmos I keep there, including a granddaughter-bestowed small stuffed platypus which is now fancied up with long, strong whiskers I find on the floor from Thistle.

• She considers it her prerogative, nay, her duty, to check out the bureau top daily and gently, tenderly, pat by sneaky pat, push all objects onto the floor — pennies, earrings, small bottles of perfume, shells, whatever.

• Even in her maturity, she still plays hide and go seek with me, scootching down to the floor and wiggling her fanny impatiently in preparation for the big leap that captures me yet again. (Yes, I still hide behind doors, couch, and bed to play this ridiculous game.)

- When I've done something to displease her, she sits with her ears laid a slant and her beautiful back to me. "Humph," is what she is saying.
- When I have company, she sits where she can be best seen, smiles serenely, and then proceeds to clean the very most nether and embarrassing parts of her body.
- Despite not being a cuddly creature (too proud, too terribly royal), she senses when I'm down or discouraged and suffers herself to sink into my lap, purring loudly and looking anxiously up at me with those beautiful, ever-so-slightly crossed blue eyes. Second-stage comfort, for when I cry or am at my wits' end about something, is to carefully clean my hands, right down to nipping gently around the nails.
- She spends the night with me, fitting herself comfortably behind the book I'm reading as I lie down and try to escape from the day, then moving as I turn the light out, to give the house one more look over, and after a half-hour or so back she comes, removes the covers gently, searches out her favorite place by my right hip and enclosed by my arm, moves me carefully around until I am in exactly the correct position for her, and hardly stirs until morning.

Oh, there's so much more. I love her. She loves me. She listens; I talk. And sometimes she talks too — I know of at least a dozen sentences. *Where's my water? Time to go upstairs. I'm so bored*

*I don't know what to do! I'm right here, just in case
you need me. What did you say?? I simply MUST
get out that door!* and more. *Praaaiiinggg!* means,
"I suppose I love you, even though you belong to
a much inferior class than I."

So Thistle is fated to survive, just as I am fated
to be her pet.

I've been honored to share my life with
several, wonderful felines, like my first kitten
Mopsy, who lived to the age of 19, and who
trained me well.

And Isis, who bore beautiful, sought-after
children for two years and then retired, and who
lived until she was 22, her last years with my
Mother, whom Isis cared for and comforted during most of Mom's last days. Now that was a
cat with a refined sense of propriety. She'd sit
in a chair and peer, ears flattened, over the table
to see if everyone was gone, then dip her right
paw ever so delicately into the glass of milk left
there, time and time again, licking her paw
between dips. And say gently, "Who, ME?"
when anyone came into the room and caught
her at it.

Oh yes, cats have been in my life forever.
There is, indeed, nothing like a cat.

A Passion for Orange

by Beverly Hall with Kate Stout

*"If you want to know the character of a woman,
find out what her cat thinks of her."*

I had vowed never to have an orange cat. Black,
gray or tabby were my kind of cats as a child, and
they were the "usual suspects" that adopted me
through the years — from Eloise (a Maltese gray
from the streets of my youth in Queens, New York
City) to a remarkable flying, leaping cat whom I
named "Cloud." She followed me on daily walks
along Tennessee Avenue in Madaket back in the six-
ties and would live out her next ten years with us.

And then, there was "Spirit," a coal black,
six-toed, all around part-Maine coon whose parents
were actually known to me. She was the only
female in a litter of five, born next door to me when
I lived in New York City. She was the apple of her
human mother's eye, and it pleased her when I
selected her favorite. But, on the day I was to take
my new kitten home, she suggested I consider a
companion to this rambunctious free spirit.

Wouldn't I like to adopt the last of her brothers — an orange kitty?

He was no competition, I thought, for my affection for the frisky Spirit, as I immediately named her. But, since I knew I would be away a lot, he might well provide both company for her and kitty damage control for me. And that was when I ate my "no orange cat" words.

I would name that cat "Saint," since he seemed one, compared with his mischievous sister. His godmother would nickname him "King Cat" for his regal bearing as a grown up. Both of us were privately convinced that Saint may well have been a dog in kitty clothing because of his faithful companioning way.

I soon became accustomed to a "big red" presence in my garden, hunting on Hither Creek, or sleeping in the crook of my arm. He lived a long, wonderful life for twelve years, enjoying Madaket.

I'd grown accustomed to my orange Tom, and missed Saint very much, so I was relieved when I received a phone call from the MSPCA, letting me know that a small, red feral kitten had arrived at the shelter, and would I like to take a look?

My husband was off-island, so I decided to stop by "just for a peek." And there he was — a new arrival salvaged from the landfill — my lion king, "Simba." I took a closer look at the tiny being; he was a bedraggled speck of orange with matted fur and a scratched up nose. I was instantly smitten.

I knew this little guy was meant to be mine, but there was the glaring problem of how to convince the human in my life of that imperative. I asked the MSPCA for some time before I committed to the adoption — to take the proposal of Cat Number Four home. I did not want to surprise Sascha with an impetuous adoption. Nor did I want to go home without that charming, long-awaited and anticipated lion of my dreams.

Convincing my husband that I was just going to take a look, he and I drove to the MSCPA. To my husband's distress and my private pleasure, on the door of his lock-up, indeed, was my name.

"I thought we were just looking," Sascha growled, "It looks as if he's already yours!"

And, in a way, he was. He was catnip to my heart.

Reluctantly, I left the kitten in the shelter to talk the adoption over at home. The new kitten was vehemently vetoed. My heart, already humming with the tuneful, "I Just Can't Wait to be King," sank.

The next day was a holiday, and, since I had some time to myself to think, I decided to go to a yoga class. I took my longing for the orange kitten and my domestic dilemma into my class. And destiny was my guide. At that very class was a friend who worked at the MSPCA.

I decided through that morning's meditation to see if she could help me bring home a holiday surprise. I had convinced myself that such a spontaneous Thanksgiving surprise would some-how dispel all doubts about the suitability of a fourth cat.

So, my friend and I went back to the MSPCA, and put little Simba into a box cheerfully marked, "I'm feeling much better, Thank You," and drove him home to hearth and husband.

I immediately shut little Simba in a bathroom and tried to assuage my deed by plying my spouse with a restorative cup of cheer and a bounteous Thanksgiving dinner. I trusted that the law of out-of-sight, out-of-mind, combined with a big meal would serve as a bridge to life with a fourth cat.

I think I excused myself by saying, something about being grateful this Thanksgiving weekend for our extended family and why not share it with one more?

My Simba has grown up to be a beautiful, orange, bull's-eye cat. He is prone to watch my every move as I dash about in my workaday mode from room to room. From the moment he came home, he has slept with me and followed me almost everywhere. And, I must compliment my husband with putting up with the loss of the share of the bed that Simba's now, larger-than-life, cat frame occupies.

So much for vows. Never say never, as it seems I can never do, when it comes to orange cats.

The F.B.I. Cat

by Beverly Hall with Kate Stout

The color of Madaket fog, he is naturally incognito. Since his earliest days with me, too, he has been a cat of many aliases, as if his business is kitty espionage. Always on the prowl, especially for fine cuisine from unsuspecting, big-hearted humans, "Ikat," as I named him, has fashioned himself many separate identities, as if it were names, not lives he was numbering to nine. "Ikat," my mist-gray cat with his white blaze and four white paws, was so named by me — his rightful mother — because his markings reminded me of the zigzag pattern of ikat fabric. I figured him, along with his sister Star, for a sure fire homebody.

Indeed, he would prove to be one of the sweetest, most gentle and lovable cats I have ever known, but it was only a matter of time before his other, secret identities began revealing themselves to me.

Before long, in our lives together, there was the first missing kitty episode. At first I thought he was just out on a prolonged hunting raid, but days stretched into weeks, and then into a month. I was set to leave the country in another two weeks, and was sick with worry by then. He'd never been gone this long before. He'd never given me the faintest hint of discontent. On the contrary, he was a dashing, attentive, lover of a cat. One of his preferred activities was to sit right in front of me on my desk on the piece of paper I was working on and stare into my eyes until I picked him up.

Four weeks stretched to five, and then to six. I was frantic with worry, on the verge of thinking that the worst had happened. With my suitcases packed for China, and my heart burdened with foreboding, I consulted "Miss Mary," a good friend who lives in California with her husband and two cats, and, as it happens, considers herself a "kitty psychic."

By fax, Miss Mary sent me a cartoon of a cat driving a car. Beneath it, she had written: "Ikat driving home to say good-bye to his Mom." I was so upset, I shredded the fax, misunderstanding the good-bye (to China, not to life on this planet) as she had intended it. The next day, around midnight, Ikat stormed into our bedroom, meowing as if it had been I who had vanished, and he was scolding me for it.

I was so startled to see him, hear him, that at first I thought I was imagining him. It was like seeing a ghost and all I could manage was to repeat his name for the first few minutes of disbelief. But our glorious reunion reassured me instantly that indeed, my wandering cat was back.

Ikat, wherever he had been, whatever he had survived, all those weeks had done so without benefit of identification. Worried that I was about to leave and he might disappear again, I wasted no time looping a collar around his neck, one that had his phone number emblazoned on it.

A neighbor called within the hour. "Your collar is on the cat I adopted this Summer," he said, as if to suggest, "Who do you think you are putting your phone number on our cat?" I rushed the mile to his house, and there was Ikat, looking doubly well-fed and unperturbed.

"We've been calling him 'Buddy'," Ikat's surrogate owner revealed. "We thought he was a stray."

Home again, I now knew that Ikat was a traveling man. He suffered form kitty wanderlust, bad. He was a goner — no matter how I tried to mark him, how I tried to love him into staying put — it was just a matter of time until he was gone again.

Another Summer, he took off for most of August. Again, I had to go away for a week, and when I returned on Labor Day, he still was not back. Again, my heart sank. No matter how many times he went AWOL nor how many joyous reunions we shared, I could never get used to his absences. This time, I put a notice in the Madaket newsletter saying he was missing, and knowing that it would go to every home in Madaket, I was certainly hopeful for some clue of his whereabouts.

Twenty-four hours, before the letters could have even been received, he sauntered in of his own free will. No one had spotted him, no one had recognized him, no one had turned him in. He simply seemed to have an uncanny knack for coming home whenever I was at my wit's end and had put out an alert. Just as he always seemed to know when I was about to leave, heading out first to beat me to the punch.

Once back, he always stayed around for awhile — just long enough to lure me into a sense of false security. Another time, again as I was preparing to leave myself, this time late in Summer for the Autumn semester of graduate school in Cambridge, he was gone again. I fretted and sweated. Miss Mary, our prestigious and accomplished kitty psychic, counseled me to simply trust him to return. But it can be hard to have faith in a creature now so famously fickle.

Where was Ikat? or Buddy? or whoever he was now?

As Columbus Day neared, there still was no sign of him. One day, my assistant in Nantucket got a call. It was a woman who had noticed — finally noticed — a telephone number of a particular gray and white kitty she had been feeding all those many weeks. About to leave the island and worried about the future of this "stray," she had, on closer kitty inspection, been able to discern the last four digits on the collar. She then called the MSPCA, already long familiar themselves with Ikat's wandering ways, for help, and they knew immediately whose cat he was.

And so she called my number and spoke to Liz who told her where we lived and she reported that she would be bringing "Foggy" home. Liz contacted me at school to share the good news. Foggy, it turns out, had been lapping up luxury all that time, as I was about to find out when I eventually reached her to thank her for returning my straying, heartbreaker, of a cat.

"He just loves scrambled eggs and cream," Foggy's newly-adopted surrogate mother reported as I silently contemplated the healthy diet he gets at home. Feeling vaguely challenged, vaguely inadequate, and although slightly annoyed, yes, I certainly was less than vaguely relieved that once again Ikat had managed to return home to his real Mom. Now, if only he could get the picture straight and practice some true kitty charity which I could only hope would begin and stay at home from this time forth.

Foggy, Buddy, Ikat — F.B.I. Incognito Cat. How many more names and identities had there been? Would there be? Would he ever come home to really stay? Or will there always be the hope of scrambled eggs and cream to woo my handsome wandering guy down the next road to who knows where?

Loving Cats and Kittens

by Nantucket Junior Girl Scout Troop #995

My kitten is nice, and I adore kittens.
— Whitney Butler

The first week we had our cat, he hid under my Dad's counter in his workshop. Later, he found a puddle under the counter and he found our cat Leo!
— Nellie Moreley, Age 9

My cat's name is Clematis. I got her for my birthday. We have an outdoor shower. At night my cat climbs up on the shower and leaps onto the roof and then she scratches at my Mom and Dad's window, then my parents let her in and send her off to bed.
— Marta

My cat Ashes is very funny. She sleeps in the fireplace at night and when anyone is in the bathroom she comes in and gets into the shower with you!
— K.E.

I have two cats that are brothers, Felix and Oscar. They are like the original "Odd Couple."

We had another cat named Tiger. We lived at Cisco Beach. One winter we moved to town. Tiger didn't like living in town, so he left and moved back to the beach all by himself.

— Alison

My cat sleeps in the sink at night. His name is Tim. We took so many pictures, because it was so cute. He is so silly he doesn't know what water is. When you turn it on, he starts biting it!!

— Alyssa Stone

Kittens love junior girl scouts. I love kittens and cats. They are really cute.

My sister Cindy is active in Acushnet Cat Rescue. She has 23 cats now living outside of her house. She feeds and shelters them. They have all been tested and neutered/spayed. She has saved approximately 100 cats over the last 5 years. I applaud and support the Nantucket Cat Rescue effort.

Sincerely,

Gail Ellis, Junior Girl Scout Leader

Thank you to all of the Girl and Boy Scout Troops who support Nantucket Cat Rescue!!!

Emily Etheridge
age 6

Cleo

by Emily Etheridge, Age 6

Cleo is my cat.

He was scared when GrandMa brought him over. He came from the animal shelter on Nantucket.[8] My GrandMa went to see him. She thought he was cute. He licked her fingers. He has brown and black and white and gray fur. He has a pink nose. He wiggles his tail. When it gets wet in the rain, he fluffs up.

GrandMa liked him very much and she decided to take him to me, Emily, for Christmas.

She put him in a special cat box and took him with her, and Maggie her dog, and GrandPa on the car ferry. He was very good. Then she drove to my house.

When she came into my house, he got scared under the bed. I came in, and he started purring. I gave him hugs and named him Cleo.

Now he lives at my house and sleeps on my bed every night. He cuddles next to me and chews my hair. He bites my earrings, but little bits.

---

[8] Cleo was found in a feral cat colony at Valero & Sons Garden Center by Shane Valero, and brought to Nantucket Cat Rescue. Cleo was neutered and examined at the MSPCA, then placed in the MSPCA shelter for adoption at Christmas, 1999. Cleo has adapted to domestic life wonderfully.

I'm glad he doesn't live in the animal shelter anymore.

I love Cleo and Cleo loves me.

There's a Limit

by Caroline Daniels

The winter of 1998/1999 was cold and windy on Nantucket. It was the second winter I had spent on the island. I was becoming accustomed to the fact that the great Northeasters' throw snow, hail, and freezing rain horizontally, relentlessly, and with great force on Nantucket from January through early April.

Living through a Nantucket winter is impossible to describe to Summer visitors. The gray clouds drop a menacing ceiling over the island, the trees are blown bare of leaves, exposed gray trunks of scrub oak twist, and a feeling of claustrophobia takes firm hold. The earliest residents, in the seventeenth and eighteenth century called February "garbage month" and March "hate month." Clearly, it's a time to get something constructive done.

On the bright side, it is a time when the year-round population has time to themselves, in contrast with the Summer months, when most are operating their businesses 24 hours a day. Some of the year-round residents say that the winter is their favorite time on the island. There's a New Englander's feeling that one should put the winter spare hours to good use.

A few of us, Lisa Dias, Margaret Frommer, Cindy Gordon and I sat in my living room looking at the fire, drinking tea or wine, listening to a Northeaster' howl outside, and wishing the Spring would come soon. We were talking about our successes and failures trapping, spaying and neutering cats, and fostering kittens for adoption. We were shaping our methods. We were sharing whatever we had learned from observing feral cats on our own properties.

We were all engaged in the pilot program at the Nantucket MSPCA to spay and neuter feral cats in our colonies. We were concerned about the various winter housing materials we provided for the cats. Once we had trapped, neutered and released the cats, we provided food, fresh water, and some form of shelter for them. The aim being to give the cats a minimum existence for their short life spans, thereby, humanely reducing the overall cat population in our colonies.

Margaret, who always brought wine, poured a glass, took a sip, and said, "Hey, how many cats do you have? I've never asked any of you that." She paused. "I have five," she added chirpily.

Lisa replied, "Five indoors, more in the colony," and she rolled her eyes thinking of the number in the colony. "I have to finish catching all of those females. We don't want any more kittens out there."

Cindy nodded and replied, "Four indoors, and about twenty-two in the colony at work, but they are all neutered and spayed, now." She let out a breath of air, "I am really relieved about that. It used to be so hard moving the trucks in the yard around during kitten season." Cindy works at her family business of Reis Trucking. About 20 large trucks move in and out of the yard all day long.

"I have two inside, and about five in the outdoor feral colony that I take are of." I said, feeling lucky that my feline population both indoors and out was low.

"Huh," Margaret said, pushing the baseball cap back over her bangs, much like a ten-year old. "How do you keep the number of cats as pets so low?"

"What do you mean?" I said, a bit defensively. I was happy with my two cats I found in a shelter in England when I lived there. They were sisters and got along very well. The cats were adapting to being indoor pets, my attempt at keeping ticks and disease away from them, and they were doing well. Our Nantucket house was new and we all had all of the space we could need. It felt great. But, I felt I should be doing more for the cat population, *at large*.

I switched the subject back to the feral cats on Nantucket, putting into practice all of the business school training I had consumed as a Professor of

Information Technology and Strategy, "We need a vision," I said.

"Right, a dream of what we want to accomplish," Lisa said.

"Well, since my colony is finished, I'm ready to help other people figure out how to trap, neuter, and release their colonies, get more people doing the same thing," Cindy said.

"Do you think we could do the whole island?" Margaret asked. "Wouldn't that be great, spaying and neutering the whole island?"

"Getting the whole population to reduce over time. Great idea!" Lisa said.

"Cool." said Cindy.

"Okay, so that's our vision," and I wrote it down on a paper and showed it back to them, "To spay and neuter the whole feral cat population of Nantucket."

"WOW!" said Lisa. "Just like that."

"Well, now we have to figure out how we are going to do it," I said. "Do you all think it is possible or do you think this is Nantucket winter thinking?"

"Hey, let's give it a try!" Lisa said with characteristic enthusiasm. "Why not?"

"Great!" said Margaret.

"Okay," I nodded.

The rest of the evening we talked about how to accomplish the vision with the whole community being able to be involved. We talked about the veterinary services we would need, the equipment, how much time it would take. By the end of the evening we were elated, but we were tired, and a little daunted by the size of the task. Although we felt it would be possible to reduce the feral cat population, we had all had experience in both business and charity work, and we knew there is a fair distance between declarations and actions.

Lisa and Margaret finished the wine, while Cindy and I tapped our tea cups, we'd done enough for one evening.

My calico cat walked by, looking at all of us, giving us a nod. We laughed.

Margaret asked me again, "how many cats did you say you have?"

"Two." I replied.

"Just two?" she asked.

"Yes," I answered, getting just slightly irritated, I was tired.

Margaret kept talking, "I mean, Jeesh, How do you keep it to two?"

"Well, how many do you have?" I asked again.

"Five."

That sounded like a huge number to me. I remember thinking, five cats is a lot of cats. "Discipline." I answered in what I knew was a bit of a smug tone, but I continued, "I just made a decision and I stick to it."

"Wow," said Margaret. "I'm impressed."

"Yes." and I could feel something echo in my

mind. That sort of distant knell, a foreboding of some sort, and I knew, definitely, that fate was laughing. I could hear it, faintly, and I ignored it.

A friend called up and said that there was a kitten wandering around in the snow and it looked injured. She was a very gentle person and sounded very upset. Would I come by and help figure out what to do? Sure.

When I arrived, there was a gray and white kitten sitting happily inside her shop. "I think she is from the colony, but she is wandering out there alone." Ginna said patting the little kitten who by now was purring. "I don't want to leave her outside. The temperature is dropping and there's a snow storm coming this weekend."

She was right, another Northeaster was about to batter the island, in fact, two were lining up to take turns over the next few days.

"I'd take the kitten home, but I want to talk it over with my husband first," Ginna said, "Would you take her for the weekend?"

Sure.

Unfortunately, after the weekend, her husband did not think another cat in their household would be a good idea, but my two and one-half year old son, who had named the kitten Twinkle, did. So, Twinkle had a home.

Three, I thought, that's okay. My son was just learning how to speak, and he said, "Daddy has Coco kitty, Mom's kitty is Lily, and my kitty is

Twinkle." Happiness. A cat for each of us and the family was complete, I thought.

During the summer of 1999, we started the Nantucket Cat Rescue project in earnest. The Nantucket MSPCA said that they would try to have the capability of spaying/neutering up to fifteen cats a week. That was generous, given the fact that their work schedules already called for long hours and dedication. They were committing themselves to adding a great deal of work to their day.

We went to work. We trapped everywhere we heard of a colony with a person at the location who would help. People called in with locations of cats, offered to trap and transport the cats to the MSPCA, release them after they were operated on, and to feed and water them when they were released. The real success of this program is due to the involvement of everyone who helped us locate cats. It's a true, grass roots effort.

And it was fun. Everyone involved knew we were helping animals that were in trouble. By spaying and neutering the cats, we knew that their health would improve, their bodies would be less stressed, and the numbers of feral cats would go down. We exhausted ourselves, and we were happy about it.

The kittens we found were fostered by many volunteers and it was rewarding to see a kitten that had little chance of a life with quality become an affectionate, purring domesticated kitten that would be adopted and have a long, high quality life before him or her.

I fostered a number of kittens at my house and I congratulated myself on the discipline I had at not adopting any of them. I fostered the kittens and, once socialized, put them in the MSPCA shelter, and they were adopted. It was great.

And, by the end of the Summer, I still had three cats. Discipline.

One afternoon, I brought a kitten that was ready to be adopted up to the shelter. As I was standing there talking to Judy Clarkson, Lisa, who worked on the front desk, came in and said there was a lady on the phone with a kitten crying under her porch, would I go over and see what I could do? Sure.

When I arrived at Nancy and David Coffin's house in town, Nancy was in a state. "The kitten has fallen into a hole under the house, next to a barbed wire fence. I think she is hurt."

"Does she show her face to you?" I asked.

"Yes, I've been feeding her, and she comes out when I back away from the dish."

We walked over to the edge of her property, and, sure enough, there was a little tabby face with a pink nose and white paws darting up through a hole in the ground, reaching through barbed wire.

"Well, she's afraid, but she looks more hungry than afraid right now. We might get lucky and be able to trap her quickly," I said optimistically.

"I've been listening to her cry for a few days, poor thing, and it seems to be growing more faint." Nancy said, obviously worried.

"Well, let's try putting some food in a trap and see what happens. We can wait a few minutes, she might go straight in."

"Would you like some tea?" Nancy offered.

"Lovely."

So, we went inside, where I met David, an architectural historian who had a splendid collection of books illustrating architectures from around the world. Sitting in their living room, with a cup of tea was very pleasant, but I had a full schedule waiting for me at home.

After about twenty minutes of interesting conversation, I suggested we check the trap. Sure enough, the kitten was inside.

Nancy clapped her hands. "Oh, the little cat will be alright now."

"Yes, now would you like to name him or her?" I had used up all of the names I had during the summer of fostering, I was quite happy to have anyone else name the next kitten found.

Obviously pleased, Nancy said, "Well,yes, it should be a good Coffin name: Jethro, if it is a boy, and Hannah if it is a girl."

"Right then," I said, closing the trap into the back of my car, "I'll let you know how he or she is. And let me know if you know someone who might like a kitten."

David saw the Nantucket Cat Rescue t-shirts in the back of my car. "Can I buy one of those to support the project?" he asked.

"Certainly, thank you very much," I said.

David wrote a check, taking the t-shirt. I backed out of their driveway thinking that this project was an interesting way to meet some of the nicest people on Nantucket that I might not, otherwise, have met. Nancy and David nodded and waved as I backed out of their driveway and drove toward the MSPCA.

Later that day, I received a phone call from Dr. Lorraine Marx, a wonderful and sensitive Vet, working at the Nantucket MSPCA. "We're going to feed her up for a few days before we spay her, she's close to starvation. We'll probably operate on Wednesday."

"Fine, let me know how it goes. Thanks very much." Of nearly six months of trapping, I had never heard that. We had reached that kitten just in time.

The kitten turned out to be female, and so she became "Hannah." Dr. Marx also found a few lacerations in her paws and mended those. One paw was abscessed quite badly and had to be stitched.

When I arrived to pick up Hannah for fostering, Dr. Marx handed me a small bottle of liquid. "You'll have to soak her paw, twice a day, for ten days."

"A feral kitten? I'm not even sure I can handle her." I replied.

"Do what you can," Dr. Marx said, "just try to soak that paw."

When I arrived home, I prepared the fostering cage: soft towel on the bottom, food and water, a soft toy, a playful noisy toy, litter tray. I covered one side of the cage with a blanket so that she would feel in a protected place. I put Hannah in it and she ran to the back of the cage.

How was I ever going to soak this kitten's paw?

I waited until the evening, when I realized I had to start, or the infection might get worse. I prepared a small bowl of warm water, put the antiseptic in it, mixed it around, and went to get Hannah.

Now, kittens of about eight weeks are small, little things, but they can be strong, as Hannah was about to demonstrate. I picked her up with a minimum of wriggling, and started to pat her, while holding her firmly. That didn't go too badly.

I sat down in my desk chair and brought the warm bowl of antiseptic mixture over right in front of Hannah. I managed to keep patting her and to get her right front paw into the mixture. So far, so good, in fact, impressively so far, so good.

Although Hannah was trying to go along with the new procedure as much as her instincts would allow her to, it was not to last, and I found that when soaking a very small kitten's paw, the best thing to wear is a bathing suit.

After ten days of this, Hannah and I were getting the hang of it. She enjoyed being patted, and

I was staying dry. She had free run of our bedroom and was sleeping on the edge of a pillow at night. She socialized quickly and was clearly ready for adoption.

One night before going to sleep, I said aloud to her, "Hannah, you are a great little kitten and you are going to have a great home. Tomorrow, I'll take you up to the MSPCA and you will find a home." I put the light out and went to sleep.

The next day, I could not find her. I had several appointments, and after awhile, gave up, thinking that I could always bring her up the next day, and left the house. When I returned home, too late now to go to the MSPCA, she was sitting in the middle of the bed, purring.

This game went on for three nights running. The odd thing was that I had fostered a lot of kittens over the Summer and thought that I had successfully blocked all of the hiding places in the fostering area, but I guess there must have been one I missed.

I still don't know where that hiding place is, because, after the fourth attempt to bring her up to the MSPCA, I said aloud, "OK Hannah, if you want to stay, you can stay." And she never hid again.

During the Autumn, we had several cats that had various interesting aspects to their characters, and so, we acquired Silver, Lucy, and Molly. Now, I was up to seven cats, and surely, that was enough.

Over Christmas, Margaret trapped two long-haired Norwegian Forest Cats: pink noses, long gray and white hair, white feet. Their hair was soft and their natures gentle. They were due to go up to the shelter for adoption just after New Year's, but on New Year's Eve, after a glass of champagne, my husband asked me if we should consider keeping them.

I was relieved in one way, since this could only mean that he was alright with the state of the increasing cat population in our house, but alarmed because, I thought we had enough.

"Don't you think we have enough cats?" I asked.

"But, I really like Alistaire and Madelaine." These were the names we had given the kittens when we fostered them.

Well, after all, Millennium Eve, who's going to say No? So, nine.

And then a friend of mine, Sheila, trapped a couple of stray or abandoned cats. The first was a cat that Dr. Paula Klek told me, "He's a magnificent cat, probably been living rough for a year. He's already neutered."

Jasper is a bullseye cat, a tabby with round black markings on his side. Jasper is a naturally regal being. I checked the lost cat book, but found no description close to Jasper. And he fit into the household so well. John thought so, too.

Finally, there is Oscar, who will probably be staying. He was a stray or abandoned cat, who

had been living rough so long, and was so fright-
ened, although still gentle, that it took three
months to calm him down. He's comfortable here.

So, our home is now complete.

At a recent Nantucket Cat Rescue meeting,
Margaret asked, "How many cats do you have
now?"

"Enough," I said, staring at a worn spot in the
carpet, "just enough."

"Takes discipline to know that," she said.

"Absolutely," I agreed. "After all, there's a
limit."

"Uh-huh," Margaret agreed.

© 1999 N. Caroline Daniels

See You Soon with Volume II

We hope you enjoyed reading the stories about Nantucket Cats.

Nantucket Cat Rescue continues working to support the spay/neutering and health of Nantucket Cats. Of the 200 cats that Nantucket Cat Rescue has spayed, neutered, and fostered, in the first year of operation about 85 have found homes, and the rest are in colonies fed and watered by volunteers. So, onto year 2!

If you would like to learn more about the program, please contact us at:

Nantucket Cat Rescue
P.O. Box 2857
Nantucket, MA. 02584
(508) 825-CATS
(508) 825-2287

Information is also available at the Nantucket MSPCA.

Volume II is in preparation. If you have a story, photograph or drawing you would like to share, please let us hear from you!! We would like to include your story in an upcoming volume. Profits from the books are given to the Nantucket Cat Rescue Fund.